10.95

cooking the English way

Summer pudding is a refreshing dessert for any time of year. (Recipe on page 27.)

cooking the
English
way

BARBARA W. HILL

easy menu
ethnic
cookbooks

Lerner Publications Company ▪ Minneapolis

Series Editor: Patricia A. Grotts
Series Consultant: Ann L. Burckhardt

Drawings and Map by Jeanette Swofford

The page border for this book is based on an original Wedgwood china pattern. Wedgwood, a high-quality chinaware, was first made in England in 1762 by the famous English potter Josiah Wedgwood.

The fabrics shown in some of the drawings of this book are Laura Ashley® prints. British designer Laura Ashley produces cotton fabrics with simple, delicate patterns similar to those that were popular in Victorian England. Designs are often taken from the flyleaves of old books and from old English china patterns.

To Jonathan, without whose appetites this book might never have materialized

ACKNOWLEDGMENTS: The illustrations are reproduced through the courtesy of: pp. 2, 4, 34, 40, 48, Robert L. Wolfe; p. 11, Tea Council of the U.S.A., Inc.; pp. 20, 28, 39, Burch Communications, Inc.; p. 22, American Lamb Council; p. 25, The National Potato Promotion Board; p. 42, American Spice Trade Association. Cover photograph by Robert L. Wolfe.

Library of Congress Cataloging in Publication Data

Hill, Barbara, W.
  Cooking the English way.

  (Easy menu ethnic cookbooks)
  Includes index.
  Summary: An introduction to the cooking of England, including simple recipes for traditional breakfast, lunch, teatime, and dinner dishes. Also includes a brief history of English cooking and typical menus.
    1. Cookery, English—Juvenile literature.
2. England—Juvenile literature. [1. Cookery, English] I. Title. II. Series.
TX717.H546   641.5942   82-257
ISBN 0-8225-0903-2   AACR2

Manufactured in the United States of America

4 5 6 7 8 9 10 11 12 13 99 98 97 96 95 94 93 92 91 90

CONTENTS

Orkney Islands

Outer Hebrides

Moray Firth

Inner Hebrides

Loch Ness

Aberdeen

SCOTLAND

Grampian Mts.

Dundee

Loch Lomond

Firth of Forth

Edinburgh

Glasgow

Flag of Great Britain

Firth
of Clyde

North Channel

Cows

Sheep

Dairy Products

Newcastle
upon Tyne

North Sea

Isle of
Man

Lancashire

Pennine Mts.

*Mushrooms
Berries*

Irish Sea

Leeds

Liverpool

Manchester

ENGLAND

The Wash

Fruit

Stilton

Fish

Birmingham

The Midlands

WALES

River Thames

Bristol

Bristol
Channel

Cheddar
Gorge

London

Dover

Vegetables

Strait of
Dover

Isle of Wight

Grain

English Channel

INTRODUCTION

Juicy, tender roast beef, tasty baked mackerel, rich, buttery shortbread — these are just a few of the delicious foods that make up the cooking of England. Many Americans mistakenly think that British cooking is unexciting. Perhaps they feel it is not different enough to be interesting. Though most English food may not be unusual, it is hearty and delicious. But before I tell you about British cooking, let me introduce myself and my country.

THE LAND

I am a native Briton, born in London and brought up in the Midlands, a region in the center of England. As a child, I spent my summers in Wales, where our family's summer home in the hills overlooked the sea.

Wales and England, together with Ireland and Scotland, are the countries that make up the British Isles. These islands lie in the North Atlantic Ocean off the northwest coast of the mainland of Europe. Britain has a damp climate and moderate temperatures. Though it is never very hot or cold, it is often swept by chilly winds and sudden showers. In much of England, frequent rains turn the grassy countryside a brilliant green. Beautiful fields are crisscrossed by hedges and low stone walls and dappled with golden sunshine. In the rich soil of the hills and vales, there are crops and lush grasses for grazing sheep and cattle.

Currants and fresh buttermilk are used in rich scones, an English teatime treat.

THE FOOD

Because Britain has so much good pasture land, beef and lamb make up a large part of the British diet. Sheep, especially, have always been important to the British for both their wool and meat. (The meat of a sheep is called *lamb* if the animal is under eight months old, *mutton* if it is older.) Near our house in Wales, sheep grazed on hills covered with short grass and herbs. This diet produced meat of incredible sweetness and delicacy. We looked forward to our first roast leg of Welsh lamb for days before we left our Midlands home for the summer.

In addition to lamb, we frequently ate beef. British beef is delicious, and cattle breeds such as Angus (from Scotland) and Hereford (from England) are famous all over the world for their fine meat. As in most British homes, our Sunday meal was a real occasion. My mother would put the *joint*, or roast, in the oven as we left for church. When we got back, the aroma promised a fine meal. Sometimes it would be beef, and other times, lamb or pork. Occasionally we had chicken.

The appropriate trimmings were as important as the meat. We always had Yorkshire pudding and horseradish sauce with beef, mint sauce and new potatoes with lamb, applesauce with pork, and bread sauce — a thick, creamy mixture of bread and milk — with chicken.

While joints were for Sunday meals, hearty stews were kept for weekdays. They warmed my father when he got back from work and my brother and myself when we got home from school.

Like other Britons, we ate as much fish as meat. Since no point in the British Isles is more than 70 miles from the sea, fresh fish is available everywhere all year long. In Wales, we got our fish right from the sea. Sometimes we would go with a local fisherman to fish for our mackerel, herring, and sea bass. We would stay out the whole day and go as far as 12 miles out to sea. Seabirds would sometimes swoop down and try to steal some of our catch. On a big haul, we might catch up to 100 fish at a time.

We looked forward to opening our picnic lunches and finding such treats as homemade meat pies and jam tarts to satisfy our hunger. When we got back to the harbor, the fisherman would give us as much fish as we could carry, and he would sell the rest to the villagers. We would tramp home to cook our fine, fresh fish for supper.

In Wales, the land provides as much good food as the sea. There are lots of wild mushrooms and fruits. During the summer my mother used to bake the best blackberry-and-apple pies I have ever tasted. My brother and I would collect wild apples from the hedges along a nearby mountain stream and we would gather enormous blackberries from the tangled mass of briars that was our back garden. Mother would greet us just before lunch, her hands floury from rolling pastry and her cheeks rosy from stoking the fire for the oven.

Wild blackberries, apples, and mushrooms grow in Wales.

BRITISH TRADITIONS

Back home in the Midlands, we shopped for food like everyone else. The British tradition is to shop every day rather than once a week. Though there are now supermarkets, the British cook still usually goes to the butcher for meat and fresh game, to the fishmonger for fish, to the baker for bread and pastries, and to the greengrocer for fresh fruits and vegetables.

British shoppers can also buy outstanding dairy products, including a wealth of local cheeses. The most famous are Cheddar, from Cheddar Gorge in the west of England, and Stilton, from a village of the same name in central England. The prize of dairy products is "double cream." It is far thicker than American whipping cream — so thick that it has to be spooned, not poured, onto such mouth-watering desserts as *summer pudding* or *trifle*, a jam-covered pudding-like dessert. In southwest England, well known for its "cream teas," bowls of thick cream are served with jam and rich little tea cakes called *scones*.

In Britain, teatime is a daily custom. At 4:00 P.M., Britons everywhere pause for a soothing cup of hot tea and a bite to eat. When I was a child, I thought teatime was a great occasion, particularly if we expected guests. In addition to scones and cookies, my mother would bake at least two cakes. She carefully stored the cakes and scones in tins with exotic pictures. My mother also made cucumber sandwiches from very thin slices of buttered bread with the crusts cut off. She cut them diagonally and arranged them attractively on a large platter.

At teatime, my mother served all the lovely cakes and sandwiches on her best china. As you can imagine, afternoon tea is delightfully habit-forming. Although I now live in the United States, I still put the kettle on at 4:00 P.M. for a nice hot cup of tea.

Living here, I cook American-style a great deal. But I also prepare my favorite British dishes regularly. I hope that after reading these recipes, you will want to cook them, too!

This beautiful tea table features dainty sandwiches, mints, and an elegant cake.

BEFORE YOU BEGIN

Cooking any dish, plain or fancy, is easier and more fun if you are familiar with its ingredients. British cooking makes use of some ingredients that you may not know. You should also be familiar with the special terms that will be used in various recipes in this book. Therefore, *before* you start cooking any of the English dishes in this book, study the following "dictionary" of special ingredients and terms very carefully. Then read through the recipe you want to try from beginning to end.

Now you are ready to shop for ingredients and to organize the cookware you will need. Once you have assembled everything, you can begin to cook. It is also very important to read *The Careful Cook* on page 44 before you start. Following these rules will make your cooking experience safe, fun, and easy.

COOKING TERMS

baste — To pour or spoon liquid over food as it roasts in order to flavor and moisten it

boil — To heat a liquid over high heat until bubbles form and rise rapidly to the surface

broil — To cook directly under a heat source so that the side of the food facing the heat cooks rapidly

cut in — A way to combine solid fat and flour using your fingers, a pastry blender, or two knives. Cut or break fat into small pieces and mix them throughout the flour until mixture has a coarse, mealy consistency.

grate — To cut into tiny pieces by rubbing the food against a grater; to shred

knead — To work dough by pressing it with the palms, pushing it outward, and then pressing it over on itself

pinch — A very small amount, usually what you can pick up between your thumb and forefinger

preheat — To allow an oven to warm up to a certain temperature before putting food in it

roast — To cook in an open pan in an oven so that heat penetrates the food from all sides

sauté — To fry quickly over high heat in oil or fat, stirring or turning the food to prevent burning

sift — To mix several dry ingredients together or to remove lumps in dry ingredients by putting them through a sieve or sifter

simmer — To cook over low heat in liquid kept just below its boiling point. Bubbles may occasionally rise to the surface.

whip — To beat cream, gelatin, or egg white at high speed until light and fluffy in texture

SPECIAL INGREDIENTS

buttermilk—A milk product made from soured milk

cayenne pepper—The finely ground dried pods and seeds of a variety of hot red peppers

cornstarch—A fine white starch made from corn, commonly used for thickening sauces and gravies. *(When you use cornstarch in a recipe, put the required amount of dry cornstarch in a cup and add just enough cold water to form a smooth, thin paste. Then add to the other ingredients. This method keeps the cornstarch from forming lumps when cooked in liquid.)*

currants—Small dried seedless grapes similar to raisins

curry powder—A mixture of six or more spices that gives food a hot taste

Dijon-style mustard—A commercially prepared condiment (an ingredient used to enhance the flavor of food) made from mustard seed, white wine, vinegar, salt, and spices

garlic—An herb whose distinctive flavor is used in many dishes. Fresh garlic can usually be found in the produce department of a supermarket. Each piece or bulb can be broken up into several small sections called cloves. Most recipes use only one or two finely chopped cloves of this very strong herb. Before you chop up a clove of garlic, you will have to remove the brittle, papery covering that surrounds it.

lard—A solid shortening made from pork fat

long-grain rice—A fluffy rice that absorbs more water than other types

superfine sugar—Sugar that is similar to common granulated white sugar but with finer grains

thyme—The leaves of a bushy shrub that grows mainly in California and France. It is used as an herb in cooking and has a very strong flavor.

Worcestershire sauce—A commercially prepared sauce that originated in the English town of Worcester. It is made from vinegar, soy sauce, spices, molasses, garlic, chilies, and green onion.

AN ENGLISH MENU

Below is a simplified menu plan for a typical day of English cooking. Three or four ideas for each meal are included. Recipes for the starred items can be found in this book.

Breakfast

#1 Cereal with fruit
    Fried eggs
    Bacon
    *Fried bread

#2 Orange juice
    Scrambled eggs
    *Mushrooms on toast

#3 Grapefruit
    *Kedgeree
    Grilled tomatoes
    Buttered toast

Lunch

#1 *Poached halibut
    Boiled potatoes
    Asparagus
    *Trifle

#2 *Lancashire hot pot
    Green salad
    *Treacle tart

#3 *Roast beef
    *Roast potatoes
    *Yorkshire pudding
    Green peas
    *Summer pudding

Afternoon Tea

*Tea
*Shortbread
*Rich scones
*Victoria sandwich

Supper

#1 *Toad-in-the-hole
    Fruit

#2 *Welsh rarebit
    Green salad
    Cookies

#3 *Baked mackerel
    Rolls and butter
    *Custard

#4 *Shepherd's pie
    Brussels sprouts
    Fruit tart

BREAKFAST

Why not start your day with a traditional British breakfast? This hearty meal is famous for its amazing size and variety. It can include hot or cold cereal, fruit, juice, a "fry-up" made of bacon, sausage, kidney, mushrooms, tomatoes, and fried bread—and, of course, eggs. Add a pot of steaming coffee or tea and hot buttered toast with marmalade. What better way could you get ready for a hard day's work? If this seems a little *too* hearty for you, try just one of the following dishes with your morning eggs.

Fried Bread

This is a favorite accompaniment to eggs and bacon. After you have fried the bacon, keep the fat in the pan hot.

4 slices white bread
⅓ cup milk

1. Brush a little milk on both sides of each piece of bread.
2. In bacon fat, fry bread quickly on both sides until crisp.

Serves 4

Mushrooms on Toast

½ pound fresh mushrooms
2 tablespoons butter
   salt and pepper
1 tablespoon cornstarch
1 cup milk
4 slices buttered toast

1. Wash mushrooms and drain on a paper towel. Cut into quarters.
2. Melt butter in a frying pan. Add mushrooms and salt and pepper to taste. Sauté until soft.
3. In a cup, mix cornstarch with a little of the milk to make a smooth, thin paste. Then add rest of milk and stir until mixture is free of lumps.
4. Slowly add milk mixture to mushrooms in the pan, stirring constantly. Cook over low heat for 1 minute.
5. Pour mixture over toast and serve immediately.

Serves 4

Kedgeree

This curried fish dish originated in India. During the late 1800s, when India was part of the British Empire, the British took some of India's exotic dishes home and changed them to suit their own tastes. Kedgeree (ked-jer-EE) became a favorite part of the huge breakfasts served at the country estates of wealthy Britons.

4 eggs
4 quarts water
1 teaspoon salt
1 cup long-grain rice, uncooked
1 pound smoked haddock (finnan
**   haddie), or 2 cups cooked white**
**   fish, or 2 (7-ounce) cans of**
**   salmon or tuna**
4 tablespoons (½ stick) butter
1 tablespoon curry powder
**   pinch of cayenne pepper**
1 tablespoon chopped fresh parsley

1. Bring eggs to a boil in a saucepan of water and continue to boil for 10 to 15 minutes. Allow to cool, then peel and finely chop. Put aside.

2. In a kettle, bring 4 quarts of water and salt to a boil. Add rice to water in a thin stream to keep the boil going. Then reduce heat and simmer for 15 minutes, uncovered. Drain rice and set aside in a warm place.

3. (If you are using cooked white fish, salmon, or tuna, skip steps 3 and 4.) If using smoked haddock, put it in a deep saucepan and cover with cold water. Bring to a boil and then reduce heat and simmer for 10 minutes.

4. Drain fish and transfer to a bowl. Break it up into flakes with a fork, removing any bones.

5. Melt butter in a large saucepan and stir in curry powder and cayenne pepper. Cook for 1 minute over low heat.

6. Add rice and fish and stir until well mixed and warmed through. Add half the chopped egg and stir.

7. Transfer kedgeree to a warm platter, sprinkle with remaining chopped egg and parsley, and serve immediately.

Serves 4

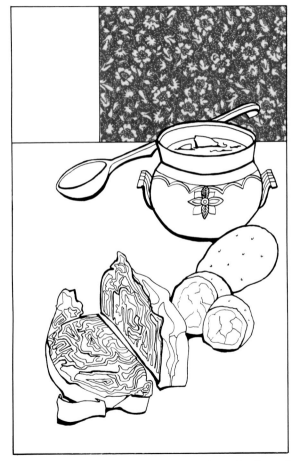

Stew, cabbage, and potatoes are often the ''meat and two veg'' of a typical British lunch.

LUNCH

The British use the word *lunch* to describe the midday meal that is served between 12:00 and 2:00 P.M. In Britain, a family lunch is often quite hearty. It generally consists of "meat and two veg" and "pudding." The meat is often a stew, and the vegetables usually include a starchy one, such as potatoes, and a green one, such as cabbage.

Pudding is another name for dessert. In England, a pudding may be many things besides the creamy milk-based dessert that Americans call pudding. It might be a pie or a sponge cake. It could be hot or cold, but most often it will be hot — to help make people warm during the cold, damp English weather.

Lemon slices and parsley sprigs add color to poached halibut.

Poached Halibut (or Haddock)

This recipe is delicious with or without the sauce.

1½ pounds (or 4 steaks) halibut or
   haddock
2 tablespoons butter
   salt and pepper
1 cup milk

1. Preheat the oven to 375°.
2. Smear butter into a deep baking dish and lay fish in the bottom. Sprinkle with salt and pepper and pour milk over it.
3. Cover with foil and bake in the middle of the oven for 40 minutes. If you are not making sauce, fish is now ready to serve.

Sauce ingredients:

2 teaspoons cornstarch
2 tablespoons milk
2 tablespoons chopped fresh parsley
1 teaspoon lemon juice

1. When fish is cooked, remove the pan from the oven. With a spoon or baster, draw off all liquid into a small saucepan. (Turn the oven down to 200° and return fish to it to keep warm.)
2. Bring liquid in the saucepan to a boil over moderate heat.
3. In a cup, mix cornstarch and 2 tablespoons milk together to make a smooth, thin paste.
4. Gradually pour cornstarch paste into boiling liquid, stirring constantly to prevent lumps. Add parsley and lemon juice.
5. Pour sauce over fish and serve immediately.

Serves 4

Many kinds of vegetables, including green beans, peas, and cabbage, can be used in Lancashire hot pot.

Lancashire Hot Pot

Almost every region of the British Isles has its own version of stew, a hearty combination of vegetables and meat cooked slowly in liquid. This version comes from Lancashire, an area of rich, fertile plains in the northwestern part of England.

This recipe works well in an electric slow cooker. Layer ingredients in cooker with meat on top. Cover and cook on High for 1 hour. Then reduce temperature to Low and cook for 10 to 12 hours.

1½ **pounds lamb (lean lamb chops preferred)**
6 **large potatoes**
4 **medium-sized onions**
4 **large carrots**
¼ **pound mushrooms**
2 **tablespoons softened butter**
   salt and pepper
2 **cups water**
1 **tablespoon chopped fresh parsley**

1. Cut lamb chops into pieces 2 inches long and 1 inch wide.
2. Peel potatoes, onions, and carrots. Slice crosswise into ¼-inch pieces.
3. Wash mushrooms and cut in half.
4. Preheat the oven to 325°.
5. Smear 1 tablespoon butter over the bottom and sides of a deep 4-quart casserole.
6. Spread a third of potatoes evenly over the bottom of the casserole. Then put in half the meat and half the other vegetables. Sprinkle with salt and pepper.
7. Spread another third of potatoes evenly in the casserole and arrange remaining meat and vegetables on top. Spread rest of potatoes evenly over the top. Sprinkle with more salt and pepper.
8. Pour 2 cups water over all. Dot with remaining tablespoon of butter.
9. Cover the casserole and cook in middle of the oven at least 2 hours. During the last half hour, take the lid off so the top potatoes get nicely browned.
10. Sprinkle with parsley and serve.

Serves 4

Roast Beef

This classic English dish is usually served with browned roast potatoes and fluffy Yorkshire pudding (recipe follows). When you shop for a beef roast, pick one that is well marbled, *or flecked inside with tiny, white bits of fat. It should also have a thick layer of fat around the outside. When cooked, such a roast will be juicier and tastier than a perfectly lean roast.*

**a 3½- to 4-pound boneless sirloin roast, rolled and tied (boneless roasts already rolled and tied are sold in many stores)
salt and pepper
3 tablespoons lard or vegetable shortening**

1. Preheat the oven to 350°.
2. Sprinkle salt and pepper over roast. Place roast on a wire rack in an open roasting pan with the fat side on top. (In other words, roast should be standing on its edge, not lying flat.) Dot with lard. Insert a meat thermometer into the center of roast so that the top does not touch the fat.
3. Roast in the middle of the oven for 2 hours, or until the meat thermometer registers that roast is done. When beef is rare, the meat thermometer will show 130° to 140°; when medium, 150° to 160°; when well done, 160° to 170°.

Serves 4

Browned Roast Potatoes

**8 medium-sized potatoes
salt**

1. Wash and peel potatoes. Put them in a saucepan and barely cover with lightly salted water. Boil until half-cooked (about 10 minutes).
2. Drain potatoes and put them around roast that has already been in the oven for 15 minutes. Potatoes should cook for at least 45 minutes to 1 hour. Baste them with fat from meat.
3. Turn potatoes occasionally during cooking and baste again to brown.

Serves 4

Juicy roast beef and browned roast potatoes make a delicious and filling Sunday meal. Serve them with your favorite vegetable.

Yorkshire Pudding

A British pudding is not always a sweet dessert. Yorkshire pudding has a light, fluffy batter and is traditionally served as an accompaniment to roast beef.

1 portion Yorkshire pudding batter
2 tablespoons lard or vegetable
**   shortening or beef drippings**
¼ cup cold water

1. Prepare pudding batter.
2. One-half hour before the meal is to be served, heat the oven to 425°. Move meat to a low shelf in the oven, where the temperature will stay slightly cooler.
3. Put lard in an 8- by 12-inch baking pan. Or have an experienced cook help you draw 2 tablespoons of fat from the roasting pan. Melt lard on top shelf of the oven.
4. Pour ¼ cup cold water onto chilled pudding batter and stir well. Then pour mixture into melted lard in the baking pan. Return pan to the top shelf of the oven for 20 minutes.

5. Cut Yorkshire pudding into squares and arrange them around roast sirloin with roast potatoes. Serve with horse-radish sauce, if desired.

Serves 4

Yorkshire Pudding Batter

This is the basic batter for Yorkshire pudding and toad-in-the-hole (page 38).

½ cup all-purpose flour
1 teaspoon baking powder
¼ teaspoon salt
**   pinch of pepper**
1 egg
1 cup milk

1. In a bowl, sift flour and baking powder.
2. Mix in salt and pepper.
3. Make a hollow in the center of flour mixture and crack egg into it. Stir well.
4. Add milk gradually and beat until smooth, using an electric mixer if available.
5. Refrigerate at least one-half hour.

Makes 1 portion

Summer Pudding

Summer pudding is especially good when made with fresh fruit. Just use 1 cup fresh raspberries, 1 cup fresh sliced straw-berries, and 2 cups fresh blackberries. Sweetened frozen fruit can also be used, but remember to omit the 1 cup of sugar.

1 10-ounce package frozen unsweetened raspberries, thawed
1 10-ounce package frozen unsweetened sliced strawberries, thawed
1 1-pound package frozen unsweetened blackberries, thawed
1 cup sugar
1 loaf sliced white bread, several days old

1. Stir all fruit and sugar together in a large bowl. (Allow frozen fruit to defrost thoroughly.)
2. Meanwhile, cut the crusts off as many bread slices as you will need to line a deep 2-quart bowl. Cut a round piece for the bottom of the bowl and several overlapping wedges for the sides.
3. Line the bowl with bread and pour in fruit mixture and juices. Cover the top completely with more bread slices.
4. Over top bread slices, put a plate that is small enough to fit inside the rim of the bowl. Place a heavy weight such as a brick or a rock on top to press it down firmly. Refrigerate for at least 24 hours.
5. When ready to serve, remove the weight and plate. To unmold pudding, place a serving plate upside down on top of the bowl. Then, grasping plate and bowl firmly, turn them over quickly. The pudding should slide easily onto the plate. If it doesn't, slide a knife blade around the inside edge to loosen it.
6. The fruit juices should now be soaked up by the bread so that pudding is a rich purple-red color. Serve with a large bowl of fresh whipped cream.

Serves 8

Treacle tart is a sweet dessert that can be served either hot or cold.

Treacle Tart

Treacle (TREE-kuhl) is the British term for molasses. In Britain, golden syrup — *a special sweet syrup — is also known as treacle. It is often used as a flavoring in sweet puddings.*

1 portion short pastry (see page 31)
2 cups bread crumbs or 2 cups
**   crushed breakfast cereal flakes**
**   (about 4 cups before crushing)**
½ cup molasses mixed with ½ cup
**   light corn syrup**

1. On a lightly floured board or pastry cloth, roll out pastry into a circle about 11 inches in diameter. Then roll sheet of pastry around your rolling pin, lift it up, and unroll into a 9-inch pie plate. Press dough gently against the sides and bottom of the plate.
2. Trim excess pastry from the edge and press the edge all around with the tines of a fork to make it wavy.
3. Spread bread crumbs or crushed breakfast cereal flakes evenly over the bottom crust. Then pour molasses-syrup mixture all over flakes.
4. Preheat the oven to 425°.
5. Form leftover pastry trimmings into a ball and roll out again. Cut into long, narrow strips. Use these to make a latticework pattern over tart. Moisten the ends of the strips with water and press them into the edges of the bottom crust.
6. Bake tart in middle of oven for 20 to 25 minutes. Serve with custard (see page 31).

Serves 7 or 8

Trifle

**1 package (16) ladyfingers or 4 large
     slices pound cake**
½ cup raspberry jam
**1 portion (2½ cups) custard (see page
     31)**
1 cup whipping cream
**1 tablespoon sifted powdered sugar
     chocolate sprinkles**

1. Line the bottom of a deep-sided,
flat-bottomed dish with ladyfingers or
pound cake.
2. Spread evenly with raspberry jam.
3. Make custard. While it is still hot,
pour it over cake and jam. Refrigerate for
at least 2 hours.
4. Just before serving, whip cream into
soft peaks. (For best results, chill cream,
bowl, and beaters before whipping.) Then
quickly beat in sifted powdered sugar.
5. Spread cream in swirls over top of
chilled custard and decorate with
chocolate sprinkles.

Serves 4

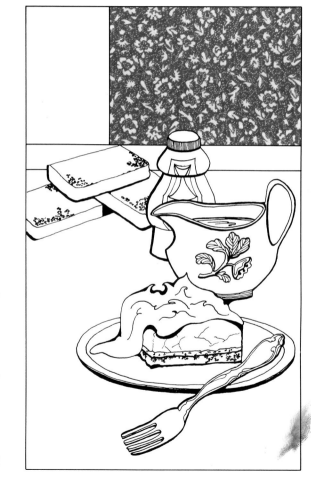

Short Pastry

Use this as a crust for sweet fruit pies and all kinds of tarts, including treacle tarts (page 29).

1 cup all-purpose flour
2 teaspoons baking powder
½ teaspoon salt
4 tablespoons chilled margarine
4 tablespoons chilled lard
2 tablespoons superfine sugar
cold water (about 4 tablespoons)

1. Sift flour, baking powder, and salt in a bowl.
2. Cut margarine and lard into small pieces. Rub quickly into flour mixture with your fingertips until it is like big bread crumbs.
3. With a table knife, stir in sugar and enough water to make a fairly stiff dough.
4. Gather dough into a ball and cover tightly with waxed paper or plastic wrap. Chill 1 hour before using. (This pastry is usually baked at 425°.)

Makes one 9-inch pie crust

Custard

This rich custard may be served with treacle tart (page 29) or on a trifle (page 30). It is also good to eat by itself, hot or cold.

2 teaspoons cornstarch
2 cups milk
4 tablespoons sugar
2 eggs, well beaten
½ teaspoon vanilla extract

1. In a cup, mix cornstarch with a little of the milk to make a smooth, thin paste.
2. Meanwhile, pour rest of milk into a saucepan and add sugar.
3. Heat until almost boiling, then remove pan from heat and pour in cornstarch paste. Stir constantly with a wooden spoon to keep lumps from being formed.
4. Return to a low heat for a few moments, still stirring. When sauce begins to thicken, remove from heat. Stir in beaten eggs and vanilla extract. Serve immediately.

Makes 2½ cups

AFTERNOON TEA

At 4:00 in the afternoon, everything in Britain suddenly seems to slow down. It is the hour for that delightful British custom, afternoon tea. Teatime can be a simple "cuppa" (cup of tea) and a light snack or a fancy affair with sandwiches, cakes, cookies, and scones with jam and thick cream.

The tea itself is usually made in a teapot with loose tea rather than tea bags. The British often make up their own blends with a variety of teas from India, Sri Lanka, and China. Britons put milk (not cream) in their tea and often sugar as well. The following pages include a description of the time-honored ritual of making tea in the British fashion as well as recipes for a few scrumptious goodies that go with it.

Tea

1 cup water per person
1 teaspoon of loose tea for each
person "and one for the pot"
(or 1 tea bag for each person
"and one for the pot")

1. Fill a kettle with cold water. Bring water to a boil.
2. Meanwhile, warm the teapot by filling it with hot tap water.
3. When water in the kettle boils, empty hot tap water from the teapot. Put in tea by teaspoonful or bag.
4. Fill the teapot with boiling water.
5. Allow tea to set for 2 minutes. Stir and serve.

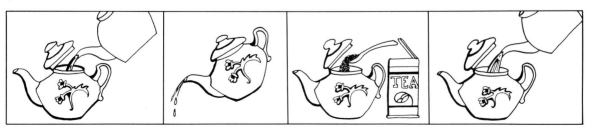

Shortbread

½ cup (1 stick) softened butter, preferably unsalted
3 tablespoons superfine sugar
1 cup all-purpose flour

1. Grease a cookie sheet and set aside.
2. Beat butter and sugar to a light, frothy cream.
3. Stir in flour as lightly as possible until mixture is like fine bread crumbs.
4. Turn mixture out onto a floured surface (such as a board or tabletop) and knead gently until it forms a smooth dough.
5. Form dough into a circle 6 inches in diameter and ½ inch thick and transfer it to the cookie sheet. Prick surface of dough lightly with a fork.
6. Place the cookie sheet in the refrigerator and chill dough for 20 minutes.
7. Preheat the oven to 350°.
8. Bake shortbread in the middle of the oven for 10 minutes. Then turn the oven down to 300° and bake shortbread for 30 to 40 minutes or until it is crisp and lightly browned.
9. Remove the cookie sheet from the oven and with a sharp knife cut shortbread into 8 triangles. Let triangles cool slightly on the cookie sheet and then transfer them to a wire rack to cool completely.
10. Serve shortbread immediately or store in an airtight container.

Makes 8 triangles

Butter, sugar, and flour are all you need to make shortbread.

Rich scones and golden shortbread make delicious teatime treats.

Rich Scones

2 cups all-purpose flour
2 teaspoons baking powder
½ teaspoon salt
4 tablespoons lard
¼ cup sugar
¼ to ½ cup currants (if desired)
¼ cup milk or buttermilk (enough to make a stiff dough)

1. In a large bowl, sift flour, baking powder, and salt.
2. Thoroughly mix in lard with your fingers. Then add sugar and currants. Mix well.
3. Stir in enough milk to form a stiff dough.
4. Preheat the oven to 425°.
5. On a lightly floured surface (such as a board or tabletop), roll dough out until it is ¾ inch thick. Cut into 2-inch circles (use a cookie cutter or the rim of a small drinking glass).

6. Place on a greased, floured cookie sheet and bake in the middle of the oven for about 10 minutes or until the tops are light golden.
7. Serve while still warm with butter, jam, and whipped cream, if you like.

Makes 12 to 16 scones

Warm scones taste great with butter and jam.

Victoria Sandwich

This luscious teatime treat consists of two layers of light, fluffy sponge cake with creamy frosting "sandwiched" in between and swirled on top.

Cake ingredients:

2 eggs
½ cup (1 stick) margarine or butter
½ cup superfine sugar
1 cup plus 2 tablespoons all-purpose flour sifted together with 2 teaspoons baking powder

Flavoring ingredients:

lemon — **6 drops lemon extract and grated peel of 1 lemon**

chocolate — **3 tablespoons cocoa mixed with enough water or milk to make a stiff paste**

coffee — **1 heaping tablespoon instant coffee mixed with 1 tablespoon boiling water**

1. Mix flavoring of your choice in a cup and set aside.
2. In a bowl, beat eggs with an electric mixer until frothy.
3. In a larger bowl, use the mixer to beat margarine and sugar until light and frothy.
4. Add a little egg to margarine/sugar mixture and beat well. Add a little flour and beat. Repeat alternate additions of egg and flour, beating constantly until all is well blended.
5. Preheat the oven to 375°.
6. Add flavoring and beat well.
7. Take two 7-inch cake pans about 1½ inches deep and grease the bottoms and sides with margarine. Follow this with a light dusting of flour, shaking out any excess. Line the bottom of each pan with a circle of waxed paper to prevent sticking.
8. Spoon equal amounts of cake mixture into each pan and spread evenly with a rubber spatula. Make the center a little lower than the sides because the center always rises more.
9. Bake cakes in the middle-to-upper part

of the oven for 20 minutes or until their edges come away from the pans.

10. Remove from the oven and allow to cool for 10 minutes in the pans. Then tip cakes onto a wire rack to cool completely.

Frosting ingredients:

**1½ cups powdered sugar
4 tablespoons (½ stick) margarine**

Flavoring ingredients for frosting:

lemon — **6 drops lemon extract mixed with a little lemon juice and grated peel of half a lemon**

chocolate — **1½ tablespoons cocoa sifted together with the powdered sugar and mixed with a little water**

coffee — **1 teaspoon instant coffee mixed with a little hot water**

1. Mix flavoring to match cake and set aside.

2. Beat sugar and margarine together with an electric mixer until completely smooth. Then add flavoring and beat well.

(For chocolate frosting, you will already have mixed sugar into flavoring. So now beat flavoring and margarine together.)

3. To assemble cake, remove the waxed paper. Place one cake bottom-side up on a serving plate and spread the top with half the frosting.

4. Place other cake right-side up on top and press gently. Then spread the top with remaining frosting.

5. The cake's flavor will improve if it is kept in a cake tin for a couple of days before serving.

Serves 10

SUPPER

In Britain, supper can be any meal eaten from 6:00 P.M. to late at night. Only a very formal meal eaten rather late would be called *dinner*. If supper is eaten very early (before 6:00), it might be called *high tea*. It would include a combination of tea and supper dishes. But usually people eat supper between 6:00 and 7:00 P.M.

Supper consists of a main dish, which is generally not as hearty as the lunchtime main dish, and a dessert. After dessert, the British sometimes have cheese and crackers. Coffee is never served with dessert but is served afterwards, either at the table with the cheese and crackers or by itself in the living room.

Toad-in-the-Hole

1 portion of Yorkshire pudding batter (see page 26)
1 pound pork links or precooked sausages
¼ cup cold water

1. Make batter as explained on page 26 and refrigerate for one-half hour.
2. Meanwhile, preheat the oven to 425°. Cut sausages in half and place them in an 8- by 12-inch baking pan. Cook in the middle of the oven for 20 minutes. (Heat precooked sausages only briefly before adding pudding batter.)
3. Stir ¼ cup cold water into chilled batter and pour batter over sausages. (Do not drain the fat from the pan.)
4. Bake for another 30 minutes. (Batter will puff up and turn golden brown on top.) Cut into portions and serve immediately.

Serves 4

Toad-in-the-hole is a tasty and economical supper dish.

Bubbling hot Welsh rarebit can be served for a light meal or for a snack.

Welsh Rarebit

This tasty dish is also known as Welsh Rabbit. Some people say that when hunters in Britain returned home from the hunt without a rabbit, this is what they ate for supper!

4 slices toast
8 ounces Cheddar cheese, grated (2 cups when grated)
2 tablespoons Dijon-style mustard
2 beaten eggs
4 tablespoons whipping cream
1 teaspoon Worcestershire sauce pinch of cayenne pepper

1. In a bowl, use a fork to blend all ingredients except toast.
2. Preheat the broiler. (Cover the surface of the broiler pan with foil to keep hard-to-clean melted cheese from sticking to it.)
3. Divide mixture into 4 equal portions and pile onto slices of toast.
4. Broil toast until cheese mixture bubbles and turns brown. Serve immediately.

Serves 4

Baked Mackerel (or Trout)

You may also use fresh herring in this recipe.

4 whole mackerel (or trout), gutted and cleaned, with heads removed
salt and pepper and juice of ½ lemon
4 sprigs fresh parsley
4 tablespoons (½ stick) butter or margarine

1. Preheat the oven to 375°.
2. Wash each fish under cold running water and pat dry with paper towels.
3. Sprinkle each fish with salt and pepper and a few drops lemon juice. Place a sprig of parsley inside each.
4. Butter 4 squares of foil and lay a fish on each. Fold the foil over and seal the top and both ends.
5. Place the 4 packages on a cookie sheet. Bake in the middle of the oven for 20 to 25 minutes.
6. Serve fish in the foil. Serve lemon wedges with mackerel and malt vinegar with herring.

Serves 4

Shepherd's pie topped with mashed potatoes is a favorite dish of both children and adults.

Shepherd's Pie

3 large potatoes, peeled and halved
2 tablespoons butter
salt and pepper to taste
about ¼ cup milk
1 tablespoon vegetable oil
1 large onion, chopped
1 pound ground beef
1 large carrot, grated
½ teaspoon thyme
1 tablespoon chopped fresh parsley
½ clove garlic, finely chopped, or
pinch of garlic powder (optional)
salt and pepper to taste
1 tablespoon soy sauce

1. Cook potatoes in 2 quarts boiling, salted water until soft (about 15 to 20 minutes).
2. Drain off water and add butter, salt, and pepper. Mash potatoes, adding enough milk to make a smooth mixture. Set aside.
3. Heat oil in a large skillet and sauté onion until soft. Stir in ground beef and then add carrot, thyme, parsley, garlic, pepper, and salt. (Don't use too much salt because soy sauce is salty.) Cook for another 5 minutes. Add soy sauce and stir well.
4. Preheat the oven to 375°.
5. Spread meat mixture in a deep pie dish. Spread mashed potatoes evenly over meat mixture and swirl attractively with a fork.
6. Bake in the middle of the oven for one-half hour or until top is lightly browned. Serve at once.

Serves 4

THE CAREFUL COOK

Whenever you cook, there are certain safety rules you must always keep in mind. Even experienced cooks follow these rules when they are in the kitchen.

1. Always wash your hands before handling food.
2. Thoroughly wash all raw vegetables and fruits to remove dirt, chemicals, and insecticides.
3. Use a cutting board when cutting up vegetables and fruits. Don't cut them up in your hand! And be sure to cut in a direction *away* from you and your fingers.
4. Long hair or loose clothing can easily catch fire if brought near the burners of a stove. If you have long hair, tie it back before you start cooking.
5. Turn all pot handles toward the back of the stove so that you will not catch your sleeve or jewelry on them. This is especially important when younger brothers and sisters are around. They could easily knock off a pot and get burned.

6. Always use a pot holder to steady hot pots or to take pans out of the oven. Don't use a wet cloth on a hot pan because the steam it produces could burn you.
7. Lift the lid of a steaming pot with the opening away from you so that you will not get burned.
8. If you get burned, hold the burn under cold running water. Do not put grease or butter on it. Cold water helps to take the heat out, but grease or butter will only keep it in.
9. If grease or cooking oil catches fire, throw baking soda or salt at the bottom of the flame to put it out. (Water will *not* put out a grease fire.) Call for help and try to turn all the stove burners to "off."

METRIC CONVERSION CHART

WHEN YOU KNOW		MULTIPLY BY	TO FIND	
MASS (weight)				
ounces	(oz)	28.0	grams	(g)
pounds	(lb)	0.45	kilograms	(kg)
VOLUME				
teaspoons	(tsp)	5.0	milliliters	(ml)
tablespoons	(Tbsp)	15.0	milliliters	
fluid ounces	(oz)	30.0	milliliters	
cup	(c)	0.24	liters	(l)
pint	(pt)	0.47	liters	
quart	(qt)	0.95	liters	
gallon	(gal)	3.8	liters	
TEMPERATURE				
Fahrenheit (°F) temperature		5/9 (after subtracting 32)	Celsius (°C) temperature	

COMMON MEASURES AND THEIR EQUIVALENTS

3 teaspoons = 1 tablespoon

8 tablespoons = ½ cup

2 cups = 1 pint

2 pints = 1 quart

4 quarts = 1 gallon

16 ounces = 1 pound

INDEX

ABOUT THE AUTHOR

Barbara W. Hill was born in London and grew up in Rugby, England. She went to schools in Rugby and Oxford before attending art college. After her marriage, she and her husband spent two years in Sweden before moving to Northfield, Minnesota, where they currently reside. Hill is a professional artist who specializes in printmaking and painting, and her work is exhibited regularly.

Hill was first taught to cook by her mother, and she has loved cooking ever since. Although she has mastered a variety of European and Oriental cuisines, Hill's first love remains the food of her native country. She often delights her friends with English meals and takes great pleasure in both their preparation and presentation.